Banished

J. Malcolm Garcia

Aniela

I cared for my mother after my father died in 2009. She was ninety-two. Her two older siblings, Juan and Isabella, were also dead, as were most of her friends. She liked to sit in the living room and stare out the patio window at the woods that separated our house from a neighbor's property and reminisce about Aniela, her childhood nanny. She spoke about her like a second mother, which in many ways she was. My mother's mother died of the flu in 1929 when she was only thirty-nine and my mother was twelve.

How did Aniela come to work for your family? I asked her one afternoon as I made us lunch.

I don't know, she said.

Didn't you wonder?

No, she said. She was Aniela. She had always been around. I was happy to be with her.

I presumed my mother's lack of curiosity stemmed from the limits and barriers imposed on her bond with Aniela due to race and class. Especially as she grew older and became aware of such things. However, I was still surprised she never bridged these differences for a woman who provided the love of a missing mother. In fact, years later when Aniela needed her most and my mother was in a position to help she, Juan and Isabella abandoned Aniela to an institution for the mentally ill.

My mother never pried into the affairs of other people. To do so, she thought, was butting into concerns that were none of her business, that inquisitiveness was tantamount to rudeness. Yet she, herself, could be very inquisitive, and if not rude, certainly obnoxious when it suited her. When I was a boy, she would pick me up from school in her green station wagon with fake wood trim and on the way home would sometimes stop at a house that piqued her interest. She had an interior decorating degree from Manhattan College and was curious about how people accessorized their homes. I remember sitting in the car as she peered through the windshield at a stranger's living room without a hint of self-consciousness. That's prying by another name, I told her when I was home and recalled these moments. No, she would insist. I was just looking.

When it came to Aniela, however, someone she had loved, she showed little curiosity and grew impatient with my questions about her.

Don't pry, she would say.

I'm prying now. I want to know why my mother, Juan and Isabella forsook Aniela. She was a woman I never knew except through my mother's anecdotes, but those warm memories never extended beyond her childhood, long before she and her siblings shunned Aniela.

After my mother and I finished eating, I took our plates to the kitchen. She resumed staring out the window and remembered:

Stepping out of the tub, six years old and dripping water, Aniela wraps a white towel around me. I shiver against a breeze coming in the bathroom window. Hold still, she says. I shake water out of my hair, feel the strands of it slap, slap, slap around my face, and I start laughing when Aniela makes a face and turns her head a bit so the water won't get in her eyes. She holds my head, rubbing my hair with a towel until I feel my scalp grow hot. Long after you were gone, Aniela, I read somewhere how one's hair should be allowed to dry on its own; burnishing it with a towel only weakens the roots. My hair started to fall out in my fifties, Aniela. John Wayne advertised some kind of rinse, a concoction of egg and beer that was supposed to stop the shedding. Oh, how you would have laughed watching me pour that goop over my head!

Malcolm made chicken and rice this evening and I remember the summers in Puerto Rico. We raised chickens. I had never occurred to me that one day we'd eat them. The first time I noticed one of them gone, you told me the cook had butchered it for dinner. We stood in the kitchen, the curtains over the sink open to the sun. There in the sink, the dead bird slumped naked, one eye wide open to the sky as if it was observing the clouds. You stepped out for a moment. I watched you go and then I took the bird by the neck and went through a back door to the yard. A stucco fence divided our property from the neighbors. I heard their dog barking in the shadows, the rope tied to its neck dragging through fallen palm fronds. I buried the chicken with my hands and told no one where, only that I had taken it and they never should have killed my *chicken. Aniela, you and Poppa begged and begged for me to tell you what I had done with it. Poppa was sure dogs would find it. But I would not tell you. I don't recall what we ate that night, but it was not chicken.*

My mother was born in Santurce, Puerto Rico, to wealthy Spanish and Puerto Rican parents. She grew up there and in New York City, where her father practiced law. Aniela began working for her family in 1912 when her brother Juan was born. Aniela was fourteen and from Barbados. At the time, U.S. agencies recruited young girls as nannies from poor nations in the Caribbean, Mexico, and Central and South America. Being a nanny was seen as an opportunity to escape poverty.

One year, Aniela made plans to return to Barbados at the same time my then eight-year-old mother and her family prepared to leave New York by ship for a summer in Europe. My mother recalled hugging Aniela goodbye, weeping at the thought she would never see her again. When they returned three months later, however, Aniela was on the dock waiting for them. My mother rushed down the gangplank and embraced her. Years later, from comments she overheard her parents make, she learned that Aniela had returned to Barbados to meet a man whom her parents had arranged for her to marry. The wedding was canceled, however, and Aniela came back to New York. My mother never asked what happened just as years later she would never inquire about Aniela after she had entered a mental hospital. Perhaps her parents told her not to pry.

After she graduated from college, my mother stayed in New York and lived in an apartment on East 78th Street. Her father covered the rent, and Aniela cleaned and did her laundry. My mother met my father during World War II. They married in 1947. Their wedding album has two photographs of Aniela. In one, she wears a black hat. Glasses perch on her nose and her smile shows a missing tooth. She has a hand on my mother's right elbow. The fingers of her other hand curl around a purse and a pair of white gloves draped across it. My mother rests a hand on Aniela's left arm. They face away from each other. My mother stares into the camera. The expression on her face seems to be saying to the photographer, Is this all right? Aniela looks past her as if she sees someone she recognizes.

A photo on the next page shows Aniela behind my father's mother. Aniela smiles into the camera but my grandmother wears a grim expression, her shoulders slumped forward. She may not have been happy about the wedding. My mother described her as domineering. Grandmother stayed with my parents the first year of their marriage. My father did not object to her influence until my mother put her foot down, as she liked to say, and told him he had to choose between her and his mother.

My parents left New York for Chicago, where my father was vice president of the Midwest branch of Perfecto Garcia Cigars. His father had started the company in Cuba at the turn of the twentieth century. He later moved it to Tampa, where my father grew up. He had an older brother, Manuel, and two older sisters, Louise and Jo. In Chicago, my parents rented a duplex on Belmont Avenue. My brothers, John and Tom, spent their early years there. By 1957, when I was born, my parents had moved to a suburb north of the city.

My maternal grandfather died in 1955, and Aniela became unmoored. She had been his employee for forty-three years. She drifted. She visited my parents in Chicago and helped with John and Tom. John remembered Aniela as an elderly black woman who stayed for a few months at a time. Tom had no memories of her other than she made wonderful buttermilk pancakes. I do not remember her at all. In Illinois, segregation in public accommodations had been outlawed in 1885, but it was still a norm when John was born. Aniela entered my parent's apartment building through a back door, and she used a blacks-only elevator. That's just how things were in those days, my mother said. She opposed the civil rights movement, believing that social issues should be left to the states. Both she and my father thought it ridiculous when black people insisted on being called black in the 1960s. It took time for them to stop referring to them as negroes.

My father's family disdained black people. I remember going to restaurants with them in the 1960s and early 1970s when we flew to Tampa for spring break. Manuel would shout to black waiters, Boy, bring me some tea. Boy, where're our menus? Boy, what's the special today? I never heard my father say anything derogatory about black people. He left Florida at eighteen and attended the University of Wisconsin in Madison. After he graduated, he enrolled in the graduate business school at Harvard University. His life outside of Florida may have influenced his attitudes towards black people, although at the time, the late 1930s, I cannot imagine he encountered many people of color at either college. He did not express shock or dismay when in my mid-twenties I lived in San Francisco with a black roommate. He did comment on his height. He's a tall boy, he said.

Aniela would also stay with Isabella and her husband, Diego, in Mexico City. They had three boys: Carlos, Luis, and

Adrian. Carlos, now almost eighty, told me in an email, I have a very vague recollection that Aniela had somewhat of a British accent. She was an older woman when I knew her, of slender build but physically strong. She doubled as a kind of part-time nanny for us when my mother visited Puerto Rico. She was strict but in a good way. I do remember my mother saying that she had been her nanny as a child. My recollection is that my mother had kind feelings toward her. I don't know much else. From the circumstances mentioned, she must have been living in Puerto Rico or nearby. She must have been retired from work, to judge from her age. I know nothing of her economic circumstances or family relationships.

Carlos's younger brother Luis had only distant memories of her: I seem to remember that she came down to Mexico for a few months to help our mom with us when we were children. That's all.

My cousins grew up in a large, two-story house with many rooms. I remember a Maya woman, Akna, who, like Aniela, had begun working for their family when she

13

was fourteen and Carlos was a baby. She had been born in a poor village outside of Mexico City and most likely worked for my aunt for the same reason Aniela worked for my mother's family.

I can see Akna now in a gray, stained dress with a white apron. She would climb a curved staircase two steps at a time to the second-floor living room. Isabella, Diego, and my cousins barked orders at her. She would nod and in breathless voice say, *Si señora, Si señor*, and hurry off to do whatever they had asked. She had a small room on the first floor at the back of the house. A narrow cot took up most of the space.

One year when I was twenty-four, I spent the summer with Isabella. I spoke to Akna in her room and practiced my Spanish and watched her make tacos on a hotplate. She laughed easily at my mistakes and corrected me. She struck me as a little shy. Or perhaps she was nervous. No one in the family ever spent time with her. If she was needed, they called her on an intercom. A chauffeur about my age also worked for Isabella and Diego. His name was Ernesto.

One afternoon, I went with him on an errand. We stopped on the way home and watched a soccer game. Isabella later scolded me for fraternizing with the help and took Ernesto to task.

Diego suffered from manic depression now known as bipolar disorder. In December 1982, about six months after I had returned from Mexico, he died by suicide. Carlos, out for a jog, stopped by the house and found him in the bedroom dead from a self-inflicted gunshot wound. For months after his death Isabella could not sleep alone. Akna stayed with her at night. Isabella would shout, Diego, in her sleep and Akna would awaken her *Shh, señora shh. Está bien, está bien.*

Time passed. Isabella recovered from her shock and grief and could reminisce about Diego without crying. One time I asked her, Do you remember when you were visiting my parents and you wanted him to stay in bed because he had a cold and instead he got up and started jogging back and forth down the hall in his pajamas and robe with a thermometer in his mouth? Yes,

yes, she said and laughed. When it was time for lunch, Isabella told Akna to make us sandwiches. *Si, Senora*, she said in a hurried, breathless voice. As far as I was concerned there was no need to rush but she hastened to the kitchen. After decades of working for my aunt, she knew better than me what was expected of her. By then, she had resumed sleeping in her own room.

My cousins never expressed any affection for Akna. They had known her from infancy but they displayed no sense of attachment or any kind of warm feeling that I saw. They snapped orders with overbearing impatience as if she were a barely tolerable burden, and they spoke of her as one would of a reliable but flawed employee who required great forbearance and endless instruction. After Diego and Isabella died, my cousins provided her with a severance package they said was large enough to provide for her for the rest of her life. Luis called her from time to time to inquire about her well-being. After a few years, he stopped calling.

My mother, interestingly enough, was appalled by this. Akna practically raised all of them, she said.

My mother died in 2015; the house she shared with my father and where my brother and I were raised sat unoccupied while we cleared it of furniture, clothes, books, and heaps of photos and magazines and other things that fall into the general, ill-defined category of "stuff," the detritus of my parents' sixty-two-year marriage. The wood paneling of the living room, the green shag carpet of the second floor, the red-tile of the front hall, the bathroom fixtures, everything dated back to 1957, the year it was built. My parents refused to use cellphones or computers. Like the house, they had become relics of another era. Framed photos in the front hall included my grandparents, aunts and uncles from both sides of the family, but not Aniela.

One afternoon, Tom asked me if I wanted a blue couch and a square end table in the living room. When we were sick and stayed home from school, our mother would put a sheet on the couch and we would spend the morning watching *Password* and other television shows.

I don't like it, I said.

Neither do I, he said. I think we could sell that. People like retro. Do you want that? he asked about a wooden dinner table.

Looking at the table, I remembered how our father would shake salt over his food so vigorously that it sprayed across the table like birdseed. I saw stains where one of our cats coughed up fur balls, pale rings where my mother had placed potted plants dripping water. My brothers and I did our homework on this table. The wood shone from years of propping our elbows on it.

I might take it, I said.

I'd get it refinished, Tom said.

Then it wouldn't be the same.

Tom shook his head. Like my father, he was not sentimental.

I'd get it refinished, he repeated.

Behind the table, I discovered a cabinet filled with envelopes stuffed with old photos. Some of the pictures had been taken 100 years earlier, according to dates scrawled on the back. Many were riddled with holes while the sun had bleached others.

Perhaps my parents had intended to someday frame and display them. I could imagine my father stashing the photos to get them out of the way. Or perhaps my mother bundled them and put them in the cabinet so he would not discard them.

I found one photo that showed my mother, Isabella and Juan as children beside their mother. They sat in the front seat of a car, casting sidelong glances, presumably at the photographer. Staged scenery of a tree with white flowers and a hill in the distance rose behind them. Perhaps they were at a Coney Island studio that my mother said they had visited as children. Aniela sat in the back seat.

She, too, is staring off to the side. She wears a white coat and her hands are folded on her lap. All five of them looked stiff and self-conscious.

A date on a second photo read July 1918, one year after my mother's birth. Aniela kneels in a garden surrounded by large, leafy plants and white flowers. A two-story house towers above her. Laundry hangs off a line from the porch. Aniela has on a white gown and looks into the camera, her brow furrowed against the sun. Her short, dark hair catches the light. She holds a baby in her lap, maybe my mother. A white bonnet wreaths the infant's face. *Stamford, N.Y.*, someone wrote at the bottom of the photo. I remembered my mother telling me that my paternal grandfather rented a house there in the summer. Aniela cleaned his office and helped look after the children.

In the late 1950s, Aniela moved in with her sister in Brooklyn and stopped visiting my parents and Isabella and Diego. Her sister complained that Aniela was talking to herself and exhibiting other peculiar behaviors like shuffling papers and opening and closing cabinets and picking up the telephone receiver repeatedly for no reason. It scared her, she told my mother. She asked for money so she could take her to a doctor. She also spoke to Juan and Isabella. I do not know if they offered to help but I know my mother did not. Aniela's behavior grew increasingly bizarre. Eventually, her sister committed her to a state-run psychiatric hospital.

At that time, such facilities took poor patients and were known for their unsanitary, warehouse conditions. They were understaffed and underfunded compared with private hospitals which served mostly white people. Patients suffered a variety of mental health problems and misdiagnosis was common. Schizophrenia and forms of mania were less frequently diagnosed in white patients than black patients who were then also hospitalized longer and physically or chemically controlled more frequently than white patients. Aniela hated living there. She pleaded with my mother, Isabella, and Juan to talk to her sister and get her release.

My father warned against getting involved. This was a matter between Aniela and her sister, he told my mother. Aniela would be worse off in a private facility. White doctors and staff would resent a black patient and treat her poorly. It would also be very costly. As bad as it may be, she was safer where she was. My mother did not object. Neither did Juan nor Isabella.

I thought your father knew best, my mother explained to me. That's just how things were handled in those days.

Over the years, my mother wondered if Aniela had suffered from dementia or possibly Alzheimer's disease. She never spoke to her doctors. She did not remember the name of the hospital. Aniela's sister called when she died sometime in the early 1960s. My mother did not attend her funeral. She did not know the date of her death or where she was buried.

After I graduated from college, I moved to New York under the erroneous impression I had acting talent. I auditioned for plays without success and worked temp jobs. At the end of the day, I would take the D train to Brooklyn and walk five blocks to my apartment in a brownstone on Cumberland Street between Green and Lafayette Avenues. I found the apartment through an ad in *The Village Voice*. My mother told me Aniela had lived on Cumberland with her sister. She didn't remember the address.

Other brownstones dating back to the 1940s stood on both sides of the street, and on overcast days the worn buildings appeared to slump beneath the weight of gray skies. Discarded furniture and trash covered the cracked sidewalks. Tree roots snaked through the broken pavement.

Piles of sawdust and stacks of tools filled the front hall of my brownstone, and the carpeting had been torn off the staircase that led to my second-floor apartment. A handyman, Virgil Chance, had been hired by the landlord to rehab the interior but it was a chance in a million if he ever showed up.

My apartment had bay windows and the sun warmed the room on winter days. A broken-down fireplace took up the front room, which also included a kitchen. Chunks of ceiling plaster filled a bathtub. My first night, I knocked on the door of the apartment above me and asked the black woman who answered if I could borrow a blanket. She gave me one filled with holes. I asked her about the neighborhood, if it was safe. It is if you're black, she told me.

I bought a blanket the next day and returned hers. She invited me in and introduced herself: Jean Penson. Comforters covered two large chairs. I sat in one and sank almost to the floor. The dim ceiling light left the living room in shadow and a line of white light ran through a show playing on her black-and-white TV. She offered me a joint and told me she worked as a dispatcher for the Brooklyn Police Department.

We started hanging out every night and would get stoned staring at the hazy screen of her TV. Thirty-two years old and divorced, she dated several men, none of them seriously. One guy would pound on my door every time he came to pick her up. He told her he did not appreciate a white boy in the neighborhood.

His last name's Garcia, Jean would say. He's not white.

I don't know what prompted me to think about Aniela. She has always been a mystery to me. Even as a child I wondered about her. She was present in my mother's stories but absent at the same time. I wanted to draw her from the shadows and give her the presence she occupied for me.

Now that I have, I cannot say what if anything I would have done for her had I been my mother. Would I have had the courage to help her and challenge my own biases and those of my family, friends, and community? Do I need to pry more deeply into my own life and choices instead of focusing on my mother? She did not see herself reflected in the attitudes of my cousins toward Akna; perhaps I do not see myself reflected in her attitude toward Aniela. Done well, prying might be the only real antidote to dehumanizing and discarding our common humanity but it would require a unique self-awareness I do not know I possess.

Toward the end of my mother's life, I'd sit with her in the living room at night before she went to bed. A throw on her lap, a cup of black tea on the end table. She would often fall asleep. Like an old clock, her body was winding down. Sometimes, I heard her say, Aniela.

Everything all right, mom? I asked.

Yes, she said, opening her eyes. Just thinking. Raising her head she would stare out the window at the dark evening and see things I did not. Then she would doze off again and whisper, Aniela. As if she could conjure her and resolve something unsettled.

Thank You for Not Leaving Us Alone

On a recent evening, I sat in the San Diego office of immigration attorney Linette Tobin. Her two- year-old pug, Cujo, played at our feet. I waited for her to make a FaceTime call to the common-law wife of Venezuelan soccer player, asylum seeker, and now deportee, thirty-six-year-old Jerce Reyes Barrios.

Linette stared at her computer, exhaustion etched across her drawn face. She had been awake since four in the morning, worrying about Jerce. Four days earlier he had been flown to a supermax prison in El Salvador, along with more than 200 other Venezuelans. The White House had invoked the Alien Enemies Act of 1798 and used it as a shortcut to deport alleged members of a Venezuelan gang, Tren de Aragua, a U.S.-designated Foreign Terrorist Organization. The Department of Homeland Security alleged that a tattoo on Jerce's left arm showing a crown atop a soccer ball with a rosary and the word *Dios*, Spanish for God, was proof of his gang membership. Jerce had actually chosen the tattoo because it resembled the logo of his favorite soccer team, Real Madrid.

In a letter submitted to Linette on Jerce's behalf , the tattoo artist, Victor David Mengual Fernandez, from Bogota, Colombia, wrote, *Jerce] wanted a tattoo related to soccer. We searched the internet and were drawn to the ball with the crown as a representation of the King of Soccer. [Jerce] liked the idea, then we added a rosary. I attest that Jerce Barrios is not related to any of the gangs he is accused of.*

The DHS also reviewed his social media posts. They discovered a photograph of Jerce making a hand gesture that they alleged showed proof of gang membership. In fact, the gesture is often used to express affection and is commonly used as a rock 'n' roll symbol.

Linette sought and received confirmation from the Venezuelan government attesting to Jerce's clean record. In a document submitted to Linette on November 27, 2024, the Minister of Internal Policy and Legal Security, Félix Ramón Osorio Guzmán, stated, *It is verified after reviewing the database of the criminal records office and up to the issuance of*

this document, that the aforementioned citizen
DOES NOT HAVE A CRIMINAL
RECORD IN THE BOLIVARIAN RE-
PUBLIC OF VENEZUELA.

Linette called and told me about
Jerce the day after he was deported. After I
got off the phone, I thought about how ban-
ishment of this sort was well beyond the or-
dinary understanding of deportation. During
the U.S. involvement in Afghanistan and
Iraq, the seizure and transfer without legal
process of a person suspected of involvement with a terrorist group to another country for imprisonment and interrogation was
called extraordinary rendition.

Later that afternoon, Linette sent me a pic-
ture showing Jerce kneeling beside one of
his two daughters, six-year-old Carla. A
toothy grin creased a youthful face outlined
with a trim beard. He wore a cap pushed up
from his forehead and a pale green and
white soccer jersey, with black training pants
and cleats. Jerce lived in northwestern
Venezuela, in a village outside of Maracaibo,

the capital of Zulia state, known as the center of Venezuela's oil industry. Yellow and orange colonial buildings line the narrow streets of Maracaibo, beneath the shadows cast by skyscrapers.

Linette recalled when she took Jerce on pro bono as her client. She first met him at the Otay Mesa Detention Center near the San Diego-Tijuana border crossing in November 2024. He had already been held there for about six months. He was sweet, nice, she said. Soft-spoken, sincere, but very direct. Articulate. She had the impression that he had had a good education. He talked about missing his children. He said he didn't support Venezuelan President Nicolás Maduro. The record of human rights in Venezuela has been frequently criticized by human rights organizations. Concerns include attacks against journalists, political persecution, harassment of human rights defenders, poor prison conditions, torture, extrajudicial executions by death squads, and forced disappearances.

Jerce participated in two protests against Maduro's regime in February and

March 2024. At the second demonstration, authorities detained him. He was removed to a clandestine site where he received electric shocks and a form of torture that induced the first stages of asphyxiation. Despite his ordeal, he didn't regret participating in the protests. He wanted his daughters to grow up in the Venezuela he remembered from his childhood, rather than one corrupted by the autocrat Maduro. This is dangerous, his wife, Mariyin, told him. Well, Jerce told her, I have to do what I can to build a better country for my daughters. But after his detention, he knew the police would target him. After his release, he left Venezuela for the United States.

I'm so tired, Linette said. But if I'm tired, can you imagine what he must be feeling?

She last heard from Jerce on March 11, 2025, from the Otay Mesa Detention Center. Without offering any explanation, U.S. Immigration and Customs Enforcement had informed him the previous day that he would be transferred to a detention center somewhere in Texas. Transfers created uncertainty, Linette knew. Would his case remain in Otay or get referred to a new court, one where he would have to start his asylum appeal all over again? Could he keep Linette as his attorney? He sounded nervous, worried. Very worried. Perhaps, Linette thought, he had become convinced that no one from Venezuela could win an asylum case.

While she appreciated his concern, it never occurred to her that he would be exiled to El Salvador. He had an asylum hearing—known as a full removal proceeding—coming up in April, less than four weeks away and almost a year to the day when he was first detained. At an asylum hearing, an immigration judge can order an individual's removal from the country, but only after hearing evidence and reaching a decision, and the government must prove its case by clear and convincing evidence.

Linette believed Jerce had a strong case. After she had explained the meaning of the hand gesture and submitted the Venezuelan government statement that he

had no criminal record, he had been removed from maximum security at Otay
Mesa. She had also provided multiple em-
ployment letters, including one from the
Dancy Bravo Youth Soccer Foundation, and
the declaration from the tattoo artist. Still, it
puzzled her that he had been transferred to
Texas so close to his hearing.

In the days following her conversa-
tion with Jerce, Linette began receiving tear-
ful voice messages from his mother, sister,
and Mariyin. They had not heard from him
since his transfer. Linette didn't know which
detention center held him, so she called
Texas ICE offices all over the state to find
him. Most of her calls went unanswered. Fi-
nally, someone in the San Antonio office
picked up the phone and told her Jerce had
been deported on Saturday, March 15. She
wasn't told the destination, but by then it
was all over the news that the United States
had flown alleged Venezuelan gang members to El Salvador. Linette assumed Jerce
was among them. Her suspicions were confirmed when his family sent her a news
photo of a young man sitting on a floor with

other young men in white uniforms, all of them with their hands behind their shaved heads. The young man staring at the floor, they said, was Jerce. Then on March 20, CBS News released an internal government list of 238 names of the Venezuelan men deported to El Salvador. Jerce's name appeared on the list.

The absurdity of the situation left Linette speechless. The Venezuelan government confirmed that Jerce had no criminal record. He did not enter the U.S. illegally. He did it the right way. He registered with the CPB One app, developed by the federal government as a portal to various Customs and Border Protection services. On the app, asylum seekers were required to answer questions to receive an appointment with the Border Patrol. He did that. He also presented himself on time on the day of his appointment. He was allowed into the country but held in detention while he waited to present his case to an immigration judge. But now he's been deported, based on false accusations, without being allowed to appear in court. Did the people who sent him away know anything about tattoos? The meaning behind certain hand gestures? Clearly, Linette said, they didn't.

But perhaps none of that mattered. Perhaps gang association had nothing to do with any of it. Perhaps someone in authority believed that power depends on lies, intimidation, and cruelty. Blame crime and economic stresses on immigrants, then foment public bias and hatred against powerless people seeking new lives in the U.S., so that they no longer seem human, so that they become an ill-defined, shapeless threat that needs to be crushed, along with those who support them. Perhaps it is all simply some skewed notion of projecting strength through cruelty.

Shall we call Mariyin now? Linette asked. It will be getting late in Venezuela. Yes, I said.

She tapped the keys on her laptop. A loud, droning ring blared out of the speaker. After a moment, the face of thirty-two-year-old Mariyin Araujo Sandoval appeared on the screen. She had black hair pulled back from her face and wore a loose, navy blue Tshirt. I heard children talking behind her. She had made her way from Venezuela to the Shelter of Jesus the Good Shepherd for the Poor and Migrant, a refugee shelter in Tapachula, Chiapas, Mexico for Latin American migrants. She was planning to meet Jerce after he won his asylum case.

This situation is very difficult, sad, she said in an insistent voice. It's not correct. Jerce's such a good person, a good father. He thought after he had his hearing that everything would be fine. He had hoped to continue playing soccer. He was an excellent goalie. He learned soccer from his father and made a good living. Teams were always trying to recruit him. He knew how to lead. He directed the other players, and they listened to him. He loved his family and his fans.

When he told Mariyin that he was leaving Venezuela for the U.S. for his own safety, she felt conflicted. She knew he didn't want to leave her and the children, but he wanted a better life for all of them. They had two girls, six and three, and she had two boys, fifteen and nine, from a previous relationship. Jerce treated them all as his own.

As he traveled north, he'd called and described the difficulties of the trip through Mexico. He told her the huge country made the trek feel very long. He made his appointment with CBP in Mexico City and then continued on to Tijuana, nearly 1,800 miles farther north. Despite the many people he encountered who disliked migrants and tried to take advantage of them, he always sounded upbeat. He sent selfies and smiled his wide grin in each one. When he reached the United States, he thought everything would work out. He didn't sneak in. He had followed all the rules. He had requested asylum with the app like he was supposed to. He would wait for his appointment. Even when he was detained in Otay Mesa and investigated for gang affiliation, he remained positive, but his treatment saddened and angered Mariyin. Why is this happening to you? she demanded. It's all right, he replied. If you are going to rent to a stranger, you would want to see their references, no? This is the same thing. They're making sure I'm okay. Don't worry. I'll do everything they tell me, and it will be fine. Mariyin wondered if he believed that, or if he was just trying to keep her spirits up.

A sad smile wreathed Linette's face as she listened to Mariyin. I was reminded of memorial services I've attended, where speakers commented on deceased friends, revealing a side of them I never knew—moments of generosity, patience, and wisdom that made the pain of their absence even more pronounced.

Mariyin wiped tears from her eyes and took a moment before she began speaking again. She had last spoken to Jerce on March 14, the day before he was deported. He told her he was being flown to another detention center. He called it a prison. He sounded cheerful as always. The next day she saw an image on social media of a man sitting on a floor in a crowded room in a Salvadoran prison among many other men. His hands were folded behind his recently shaved head. That looks like Jerce, she thought.

Mariyin stopped talking and stared into the camera phone at us, hundreds of miles away. I could not interpret her haggard expression. She must have been left hollow, unable to feel anything but the weight of her grief, heavier each passing day with Jerce's ongoing silence. Governments in Syria, Argentina, Chile, and Pakistan, among other totalitarian regimes, do such things. Each of them has been accused of or engaged in the practice of enforced disappearances. Under the guise of national security, the U.S. has perpetrated the same crime.

What happened to Jerce was wrong, Mariyin said after a long silence. He is a good person, a good father. He thought when he had his hearing everything would be fine. She has no idea what she will do without him. She'll wait and see. She can't make plans without him.

To President Donald Trump, she would say, Please take a careful look. You'll see he is not a gang member. He is a learned person who has never committed a crime. With her heart in her hands, she would tell him, immigrants are good people.

She became quiet again and stared into the camera. The raw simplicity of her words made them all the more heart-rending. It seemed cruel to end the call. To say simply, *thank you, goodbye, good luck.* But she had children to tend to, and I had nothing more to ask her.

I'll keep you in my thoughts, I said. Thank you, she said, for not leaving us all alone.

Linette said goodbye, then the screen snapped off like a slap and Mariyin vanished. Silence fell over us like a shroud. I shut off my recorder, closed my notebook, put my pen in my pocket. Done. I would write this up and continue on with my evening. I wondered if Mariyin still lingered over the blank screen on her phone.

Thank you for not leaving us all alone, Linette repeated. I'll run out of things I can do for them, and then I'll leave them. And it kills me.

We gathered our jackets, turned off the lights, and stepped out of her office into the empty hall. Her colleagues had left. The empty desks cast long, angular shadows. As we walked down the hall, Cujo waddling in front of us, Linette told me she was trying to find a large law firm with experience litigating against the government. She wanted to ask them to file a lawsuit for damages on behalf of Jerce and demand his return to the U.S in time for his April hearing.

It would be great, she said, if someone volunteered to help.

I followed her to her car. Traffic emerged from the slog of rush hour and raced by us. The dark sky reflected only city lights in the cold air.

Why should anyone care? I asked Linette. She stopped and gave me a curious look. She repeated the question before she answered.

He's been removed from this country without being allowed to make his case to a judge, based on an accusation of gang affiliation, without anyone determining its merit. If we allow people to be imprisoned or deported on the basis of accusations, as opposed to proof and a judge's determination, then we have done away with the rule of law.

When we reached her car, Linette turned around and gave me a hug. It starts with immigrants, she said, but it won't stop with them.

She reminded me of a recent afternoon when I had visited friends in Tijuana. After I crossed back into California, a CBP officer asked for my passport. I gave it to him. He then asked who I had seen in Tijuana. Friends, I told him. What did you do with these friends? he asked. We had lunch, I told him. What did you have for lunch? he persisted. Tacos, I said. What kind? he said. Before I could answer he stopped me. Mr. Garcia, if you don't give me specifics you're not coming back in here.

I left Linette, walked to my car, and drove home. When I pulled into the driveway my phone pinged with a message. *Oh, dear God,* Linette had texted, *Jerce's sister just*

sent me videos. Children in his town shouting mes-
sages for Jerce and praying for him. Heartbreaking.

I shut off my phone, wondering how many stories like his there were, and how many more there will be. This was the beginning of something, not the end.

That night, I knew, I would not sleep either.